I0752992

Poetsbelief

TRACY CONNOLLY

Published 2020 by Your Book Angel

Printed in the United States

Edited by Keidi Keating

Layout by Rochelle Mensidor

ISBN: 978-1-7356648-2-8

Contents

Always

Always lead with abundance
Be grateful to your soul
Never ask for anything
Be at one with whole

Mirror out your kindness
Respect your neighbour so
Never give into ugly
Of persons that you know

Always find good in one
Ignore their negative low
You are but their helper
And always let it show

Our time here is short
Shorter than you know
Keep your spirit up
And share love as you go

No need for
heights
your greatness
shines already
©tracyconnolly
16/05/20

Canada's Mourning

It was hard to hear the news today
My heart goes out to all in Canada
Even with a globe so stretched with pandemic flu
There was more to add to its hysteria

In a world locked down there in NS town
Grew fear and pandemonium of disorder
They sent their best to make high arrest
But only tragedies were looming around its corner

As the night went on the chase was high
Everyone again was told to go on lockdown
Patrols took to the ground and eyes went to the skies
No one could ever thought there would be a showdown

For it became a random spree not taught to be
With fires spreading fiercely amongst the township
With acts so cold which can't be told
And a cry for help at many a person's doorstep

Then the silence came with all its pain
A town left bewildered by its tragedies
A deadly mess no one could have guessed
The sorrow and pouring of the outcry

I'm sitting here with a heart so broken
And I'm sure all of Ireland is mourning too
We may be far away across the world so wide
But Canada our thoughts are all with you

For the love of Poetry
There simply isnt
anything finer

Darkest Hour

Did we ever think this day would come,
Where fear would set upon an open doorway
Of ragged thoughts and a wall of disbelief
Being locked down as if we were stowaways

Yes, we were in denial in trying to cope
With the sudden change of all its dramas
Our smiles grew weaker as we went in deeper
To a challenge we had never known to be

Some days are more silent than the others
It's an adjustment that we all had to make
There's no rush in the plan with each other
It's just a simple life now that one can forsake

There are moments I could sit with myself
Dreaming about different adventures yet to come
Then I would suddenly wake up to my reality
Did God really want this from above?

It's something that we all have to live with
Maybe this is just our new found path
It's not like its going to be here forever
There's no point in thinking about life like that

So it seems to be our darkest hour
Like the tick tock on the clock slowing down
But as you know, nothing in life lasts forever
So I'm just going to think about that now

If you dont fail
you will never learn

EASTER

The arrival of Jesus is born today
It's the annual birth come to stay
In this case we must never dismay
That it was known to be Sunday

Easter has that certain ring so profound
As people get excited about many things
The Lord is forgiving on this day
For the celebration of life it brings

Jesus was crucified and He rose again
It's an understanding of sadness and happiness
For Easter brings the glory to all
And he who believes will never fall

The message I believe He's sharing now is
We must have hope to stay
For He believed He would rise again
So the season of new birth begins

So if you're reading this great poem
You will feel His presence near by
For Jesus wants a nation reborn
And never give into its end

Seek
Forgiveness as
the Self Respect

Eighty Years Young

I think of my mother who has a big heart
No one could match her right from the start
A mother just knows straight from her womb
The blessings God's given her were never too soon

My mother, my angel, who's always been there
Has thought of her siblings and given her care
For she was the one who gave us so much
She made us strong with her gentle touch.

She's driven, she's kind, she's helped us along
There were days that I heard her singing a song
The songs that she'd sang to us so long ago
A friend one can call no matter what time of day

I'm writing this poem for my mother to see
She's as greatly loved as one can be
She has a great heart that showered us with love
When times were tough, she'd never give up

So I'm proud to say we've reached this milestone
For it's a great day in which she was bestowed
So Happy Birthday, dear Mother, you've come this far a long
You're the best in the world and only eighty years young

Believe in who you are not
who you were going to be

Tracy Connolly

Father's Day

I look at the shelves as I walk along
They are stacked with cards and it just feels wrong
For your not here on this fine day
Your time has passed and it's hard to say

A father so loving in that I beheld
There's always the memory that I can tell
From the click of a camera, my memory ignites
As you loved to gather and snap with delight

I can hear you laughing as my memory does pause
And for that split second, you're alive in good thought
That moment I cherish as it flashes away
For you were my father, I'm happy to say

I sit here and ponder about where the time went
It's a feeling of loss one can't expend
It's tragic, I know, to lose a father so great
But I must be happy and not annihilate

Your memory is what calms me at moments like these
And meeting your friends, I'm as proud as can be
From a joke to a story, they imitate you right
And even after you're gone, they're friends for life

So today is a good day, that I am sure
As fathers surround us while here or gone before
But mine is an angel showering me with love
As it's Father's Day and it's sent from above

What sometimes seems hard is
not impossible

Global Pandemic

The global pandemic took its hold on us
It was like lightning streamed across a world so lit
We couldn't understand the meaning of where it came from
But it was there and then the world was hit.

People gathered in their houses to watch the news room
Every channel filled the airways of this flu
We who had little trust or understanding
Blinded by disbelief and devastation too

It almost felt like a fight for desperation
an uneven chill that no one could subside
It was clear we had a disaster, not mistaken
And a certain fight for one to stay alive

As we move further into the midst of this pandemic
At a speed of light no one ever could have foretold
It lurks beyond the realm of darkness and confusion
And a story that will transcend, our faith holds

I'm writing this story in my dear back garden
Everything around me seems so clear
The species have returned from their winter nest of
cocooning and are singing and displaying fine theatrical fare

So let's be clear all around what's happening
For what it seems to me is peace and despair
We can live in our minds of global pandemic
Or we can choose to sit in a garden that lacks fear.

you are your own
Scholar you dont
need proof
©By Tracy Connolly

Grand Old Days

From Kindergarten to Secondary School
The years just flew right by
With skipping ropes and hopscotch
Being the favourite of our time
And school bells ringing
With old Mrs Clancy singing
We'd rush for the school front door
And teachers came yelling
"Don't forget your spellings,"
As we ran almost hitting the floor.
So off we hurried
With no great worries
But with a stop at Mrs Rowe's sweet shop
Where we'd count our pennies
Just enough for some jellies
And skip the way home to a stop
Mother would shout, "Get your homework out,"
As I hurried away in a pout
But they were grand old days
In so many ways
And I'm so glad to have mastered them out.

The Skies are blue
and so are you
Its a great day
So come what may

HE

For he who is tortured in the mind
Seek life and strength until one is able
He needed to go to his content of joy
For now he is somewhat unstable

His smile is but a burrow in his heart
For it chants to a life of certain way
He has forgone many triumphs of his nature
But nothing more haunts him from his past

He sits at night pondering on life's completion
For he knows not the will of it's last
He's magnified and distraught over his surroundings
For they are but a shield to what is past

He acquires and contempts to his satisfactory ways
But he's yearning to belong, to free his soul
He looks at life without new aired downing
And masterfully unplugs from his tire to face the day

He is all but human and fixed in his own contemplation
And finds nothing but insults to his dismay
For he only lies to his own connection
And is powerless to it's array

His mind is a rock of institution
neither here nor there with its wit,
but he knows that he must keep on moving
And break free from the chains remit

You can love your life now or you can wait for later

HERO

The tears will fall once again
As it comes to light of your great end
You were there, you saw what's true
it didn't bother you as you knew
what you had to do

You had to fight for your dear life
and for others too who were burdened
with the plight
The task was great, you knew that well
but you started your mission
and were welcomed to hell

You entered the battlefield all alone
You carried your weapon and signals Morse code
You climbed the tree and your antenna went up
It was then you knew you would never give up

You thought of the women, the children, the troops
the Morse code was flowing, the signal did loops
Your comrades were A Company they flanked from the right,
they got your position and came in tight

The enemy was falling to your advance
You climbed from your tree and dug in your trench
The signal kept going for your great plan,
which was to execute your mission and take the enemy at hand

You called for the planes after your situation eased
Your hand was still going on your Morse key
So you executed your mission in the Irish you know
It was smart, it was genius that you couldn't bethrow

So I sit here and write this story with glee
For you were my father and I'm proud as can be
It was an honour to know you as a father and friend
'A Hero' they now call you at your great end

You only need one
believer dont search for
others

Holly

And so it was the cat for me
Far from home and compelled to be
An innocent stranger parted you gone
The look in his eyes wasn't so strong

My arms reached out to hold you tight
I was taking you home with sheer delight
Your body was warm and fluffy to feel
You purred so softly it was so real.

A box I had placed was opened afloat
I lay you down and you took note
The scent the aroma was all you did need
You saw there a bowl attempt you did feed

We eventually arrived home singing a song
Cats aren't just for Christmas they always belong
The door swung open you ran without fear
Running behind you I jumped in the air

So life began for both holly and me
I felt so lucky it was to be
So thankyou for checking that we are ok
For we are permanently happy and remarkably gay

What he reflects out
reflects his true riches
©tracyconnollyspoetrys
18/04/20

Irish Peace Keepers

Let's start at the beginning of peace-keeping time
Where they found themselves fighting for peace
When soldiers boarded Globemaster transports
And landed down in the sweltering heat

Straight into battle our Irish were driven
No one knew the outcome to be
For those brave soldiers lost their comrades
And a blanket of mourning filled Ireland's streets

We can be proud to say we are the finest blue berets
And peace keeping force in the world
With so many missions played in honour and pride
By the efforts they made no one could hide.

From the thousands of duties by our women and men
And the longest unbroken record of any country
They're clad in the armour of a righteous cause
It's a remarkable achievement without giving pause

Both home and abroad, we are one human family
And you will not sit still when others need help
Even when the demons of the past trips still haunt you,
You would give your life for others at will

For we who are the protectors of the weak
We can be the listening ears for the small
And though many of us were wounded or passed
We face the responsibility for a world that will last

As peace keepers you have something to give
And the world shows gratitude for who you are
You align with the cause for peace and freedom
And no matter where you go, your hailed a star

The service of peace strengthens the values we represent
As a nation we inspire others home and abroad
With our pursuit for international peace in mind
We have a unique record that's the only one of its kind

To give praise to the families who were their backbone
And to honour the families whose loss was far great
We thank you for all the shared hardship
And the love that you showed for every mission they did

We are very proud of those working in combat
Those who resolve public conflict, policing and rule of law
For those are the men and the women of this country
So let's be proud of them who give it their all

Just because time
changes doesnt
mean you have to

Light to Shine

I just woke up, it seems so cloudy
The day that's about to begin
Even though the hours went so fast
It was like my world was in a spin

The day before me just seems so long
I'm not sure where it's to end
It's really hot and I've been thinking
About another's life that could end

Even though I made that early call
Just something didn't seem right
I paused to listen as she spoke
But her voice was overcome with fright

I guided her the best I could
It seemed her voice was slipping away
And at times like these, the pauses came
I knew things would never be the same

I didn't want to keep you on the line
I knew it was hard for you to talk
So I hung up quickly with a sad goodbye
Leaving myself feeling with a want to cry

It can't be easy, you're still in there
And we are not allowed in
So I pray to God that he knows
For His light to shine and His love to flow

You are your own
approval
©tracy connolly
26/04/20

Memories

When I think of all the memories held
And all the days that have gone by
I pose the thought just what I dwelt
And look for the facts and reasons why

It's weird to think the years fly by
It's sad and true and can make you cry
The forgotten seeds we've planted still grow
But with another's fortunate hand they now sow

Time writes a new line in our memories
Isn't that strange how this turns to be
A beautiful moment is raised blessed from above
To sit with yourself and honourably love

I'm fortunate to be able to write these lines
I can recall dearly of gifted beautiful time
Times when we laughed to our own charades
And joyous family surroundings and escapades

So I thank you Lord for all that's done
The life you gave me has just begun
For the memories past were so graciously given
And I'm forever heartily proud to be living

learnt to cope
using lots of
soap

My following

It's a simple kind of poetry
Not many of its kind
It's speaking just to tell you
It has your thoughts in mind

There is many a poetry artist
You could truly find
But not many of them will tell you
The feeling you want inside

So here I pose the question
What makes one happy as can be?
And the response I always get
Is just love for one's poetry

So thank you to my following
I'm so happy that you're here
You are the best of audiences
And certainly bring me cheer

Line up those problems
and head for that walk
Remember there's always
someone there for you to
talk
© Tracy Connolly

My Old Man

I woke this morning and thought of you
It's a special day as it's Easter too
My Father, my friend, my old man
You're gone not forgotten from this great land

The birds are chirping and full of flight
The air is fresh and it's dry and bright
The flowers are blooming so the aroma spikes
I've a wonderful message for your delight

So here I go with Happy Birthday Cheer
For my dad who was so dear
You're up in heaven rejoicing this day
So now I know I must not dismay

I have fond memories I clearly see
And I know they'll always be with me
I love you, Dad. I know you're near
I feel your presence and my great tear

Now don't you worry because I'm alright!
It's your birthday celebration, we must light
An Easter Rising on your great day
For a wonderful dad enjoy what may

He who fears
failure will have
regrets
©tracyconnolly18/05/20

Nature

As I sit here the river just sparkles
The branches on the trees barely move
There is a beautiful flicker upon the water
And some fish jump up with a groove

I can feel the sun warming on my face
All around me is so green and beautiful too
In fact each bush seems to hug each other
It's a feeling of natural earthed bloom

The grass seems to be worn in some patches
I'm guessing many a foot has trodden the soil
They have come to see all its enriched beauty
And they have certainly walked away with a smile

I can hear many a bird chirping above me
They seem buried amongst the trees
Their happiness resonates all that surrounds me
And the pure joy of it makes me at ease

In the distance I hear a tractor's engine
And the smell of the straw being cut
It's that sweet smell of scented vernal grass
And its the love I see in a bunch of buttercups

You can tell when nature makes you this happy
It's a gift of life that's given so free
It makes you appreciate what God's given us
And it's a reminder life is not guaranteed.

BE PROUD OF
WHO YOU ARE
FOR YOU WONT
GET ANOTHER
YOU
©tracyconnolly23/05/20

Our Time

Our time in life was precious
No one could ever know
The outcome that would be
We shared so many common interests
no one else could see
We talked of times within the service
It was easy and it flowed
For they were family always
And that's how the story goes
I never will forget you
There's a scar upon my heart
It's there because I loved you
From the bottom of my heart

A Masterpiece Of
New Life Creates
Happiness
© tracyconnolly
16/05/20

Pandemic

As I write this verse, it so so hurts
To witness this pain of immeasurable patients who drain
But they too must endure to see the door
Which follows through the wheel of life and thereafter

The wards are flooded and the stench is high
The patients look onwards with fear in their eyes
I can't quite control the emotions I feel
As it's a terrible dread and an awakening deal

But I must stand tall to this great call
And not bury my head as it's needed instead
To a pandemic unknown, a curse that's far great
That no one can stop this or race to belate

My friends are so tired, their faces do show
They hold back the pain so I don't know
But I see it abrupt when pressures do lure
It is exceptionally unkind and almost sinkingly unsure

So I think of my training, passion must flow
Patients are of the utmost importance and permanently
must know
I carry a mindset that I follow for sure
It's to help one another and leave no one ashore

IF YOU KEEP
PUTTING DARTS IN
THE DART BOARD IT
SOON BECOMES
FULL

Red Robin

I wonder as I look upon my fence
What it's like to be so brave upon a height
You project your breast so triumphantly
And with a swooping move you gallop to take flight

There's many a place you land within the garden
You always hop around quickly as you flow
You're so quiet in your sudden movements
I turn swiftly just to see you go

Your visits have made me fonder of your presence
Your colours have a beauty against your soul
I've given you a name that I've kept secret
As it's something only you and me should know.

I wonder when I don't see you on a morning
Are you leaving this place as your duty is done?
But then I insist on loading the bird feeder
And to my surprise you've appeared again.

There's a certain pattern to all this movement
Maybe a certain kindness to its wave
I'm not convinced that you're here for no reason
So I'll welcome you as long as you want to stay.

One day I know you'll leave this garden
You may just have to call on someone else
But you know there and then I'll be OK
And our moments will be time well spent.

Lifes beauty will only
happen once so enjoy
that moment

Reflection

As I sit in my garden of reflection
It's hard to believe where I've come
A moment of happiness and sadness
A reality of things that are numb

The crows are croaking loudly today
The birds are chirping cheerfully away
Yet the pangs of my heart are closer
And the joy in my spirit has dismayed

For a moment the day is so beautiful
I really don't want it to end
The sun is full of enchanting measure
The craziness of life can't comprehend

I take a deep breath to remind me
Of all things good that can be
For we must never take for granted
Our lives that were given so free

So now as I look on my reflection
I know that it's time well spent
For it's a moment of true contemplation
On a world we thought would never end

One powerful act of kindness can
lead to an explosion of good Karma
© TracyConnolly13/06/20

Someone

I never thought I'd find someone, especially like you
You came out of nowhere, I didn't know what to do
I smiled at you graciously at my first sight
You giggled back at me, knowing it was right

We made a list of plans to certainly meet again
Not even sure we'd get there in the end
The feelings of childishness were embedded in our souls
And the longing in our hearts was never to let go

Communications just seem to be constantly in the air
We were so happy our meeting was drawing near
We spoke about our aspirations, we would both fulfill
Magic loomed around us and one could not sit still

Finally our day arrived with more in-depth feelings were afloat
That swagger walking towards me something I did note
A chill just rose up through me, awakening me alive
I was so happy looking into your big brown eyes

We were so excited, our future was looking bright
Love was in the air and the feelings were so right
I knew I loved you then, I can now honestly say
As I look back on that memory being a great day

Nothing surprised me as our journey went on
Our feelings just got better and became quiet strong
There's no one I'd rather be with, that I know for sure
You're beautiful and kind, a man whom I adore

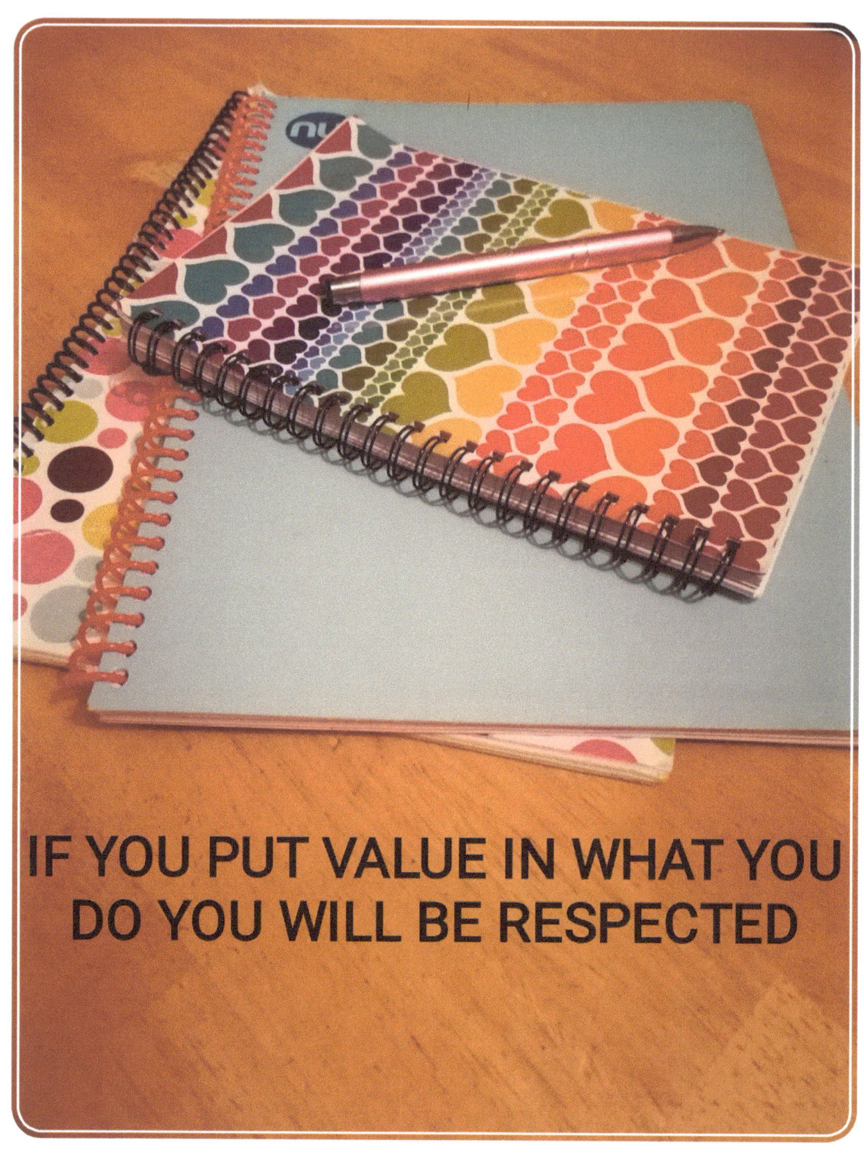
IF YOU PUT VALUE IN WHAT YOU
DO YOU WILL BE RESPECTED

The Best

Two years have passed and I won't deny
I've cried a river that I sometimes hide
I visit home and it's not the same
Your absence creates a pain
I call your name but you're not there
I see your room and an empty chair

I look around and see your picture placed
It's only then I realise what I've embraced
A lost smile, a few wise words
A dad so special, let it be heard
The memories are there, they will always be
And the acceptance of loss I clearly see

My Father was a great man, he was one of a kind
A teacher gifted in his own time
He'll never be forgotten, his memory lives on
Once was the soldier and outstandingly strong
So you see my feelings are forever stretched
For he was my father and he was simply the best.

YOU CAN NEVER LOVE ANYONE
TOO MUCH
YOU CAN ONLY LOVE THEM
MORE
©TracyConnolly20/06/20

The Bloods

It was a garrison of several towns back in 1923
When it was ordered to amalgamate during the great emergency
The southeast was then protected with their soldiers in full sight
For fear of an invasion, one must keep things pretty tight.

The 3rd Infantry Battalion under the 9th brigade rule
Situated in Boyle and Dockery Barracks became the cool
The years following the war of independence were extremely rough
But the 3rd Battalion marched on and they were never giving up

A great Officer Bernard Sweeney certainly gave good pace
As the Donegal command was scattered about the place
Upon reading the Gazette something did not fit
Where's my bloody Battalion? It's needed to commit

So around 1929 3rd Battalion finally came to be
Placed in McDonnagh Barracks in the Curragh camp to see
Training with the Lewis machine gun always seemed just right
But the switch to the Vickers made the Battalion ignite

Tactical exercises and Battalion shoots just became the norm
With German type coal scuttle helmets bringing into form
A war-like appearance, the Irish Army seemed to show
From running the Curragh plains and shouting out, gung-ho

The Bloods' huge achievements just didn't seem to end
Producing rifle and revolver teams, being their godsend
From the hurling to the football and boxing at the glow
Was there anything the Bloods didn't do or didn't even know?

Little did they predict those officers and those men
That many years on, their duties would not end
For they have seen every corner of Ireland's greatest map
From the Curragh to Flood Hall and Kilkenny to the Congo trap

With the state of world tension back in 1938
And the handling over of the treaty ports one could not
annihilate
That this was the great Battalion simply of our time
And In memory of an old soldier that will do just fine

In 1946 the Bloods saved farmer's crops
And were surrounded by people who praised them as top-notch
Their home was Connolly Barracks and they're very proud to say
The colours of red and white reflect where they lay

In 1968, Northern Ireland was troubled with civil rights
So the Bloods raised 3 border battalions loaded up in sight
It's a memory for sure they never will forget
Knowing their Blood comrades who did their very best.

Once an old Blood said to me 'Bloods will never die'
They're the bravest, maddest, funniest, humans he's ever known
And one day it will be our time to reorg
As Dílis Go Bráth you're my forever home

Heaven and Earth
There's not a day goes by that I don't think of you.
There's not a moment that passes that you don't escape my thoughts.
Heaven and Earth are so entwined as you rarely leave my mind
©TracyConnolly25/07/20

The Elderly

I think of the elderly being at home
In times like these, nobody can know
What it's like to feel the lonely road
Of age and silence with the feeling low

We wander out in such busy times
The crazy world we see enshrined
Of clogged up aisles stacking hard
No one cares or even has regard

The race is on to save the world
Yet casualties are flowing and it's absurd
To think the choice before was none
But now they choose the younger one

My gut feels tight as sickness pends
The thought of our elderly I cannot comprehend
So if you know a person of mature state
Please be kind and show your faith

A humble call just to say hello
Will brighten their hour and let them know
They are not forgotten nor will they be
For they raised this country and its sovereignty

"If you put value in what you do
you will be respected"
© TracyConnolly28/07/20

The funeral Director

You took the role for families and their loved ones
It's to be expected for the line of work you do
Your passion drives to see the most unmistakable of sorrows
And it's your focus that strives to follow through

You remember how you played your part so finely
Now it feels your offerings are some what lost
You reminisce on all your moments of your giving
And you feel your emotions are now but at a cost

It's so difficult to send the message to ten people
You're wondering how hard it will be for those to choose
It's twice the grievance for them and so upsetting
No one could comprehend what they are going through

You ponder on the fact there's no hand-shaking
No hugging or a chat to say the deceased is gone
It's like our duty to meet their needs is forsaken
And the love in our hearts is now but with a song

There's no hearse to stop upon the family doorstep
All our needs just seem to feel that they have gone
The sense of satisfaction it is but a wildcard
But inevitably it's made us very strong

My thoughts dwell upon the family
To celebrate one's life so young and old
The Irish really got it so strong and together
They always had the celebration of life to the fold

I'm looking at a great community that came to the fore
The door would open and the cakes would but arrive
The people would gather making sure the jobs are done
It's a certain kind of comradeship once it's all begun

It's uncanny the feeling that I will forever hold
It's a systematic world who's not holding to its bond
So turn off the lights and we will so remember
The honour guard in which they belong

you are here for a reason
not a bad one

The Heartache Within

I felt the heartache of my friend
It hurt me deeply, I could not comprehend
The pain and grief you held within
I asked the Lord, "Has this man sinned?"
For the pain on this one person was so great
That I felt myself this cannot be faith
He looked at me with his big blue eyes
I knew this couldn't possibly be a disguise
He told me little but I felt I knew
I didn't have to be convinced his pain was true
He told me of the Sisters' faith
He told me he went and they opened the gates
His time spent there in that holy place
It made him think about his own grace
A shattered man, what could they do
But pray for him and his son too?
The darkest hours, the Sisters prayed
Because they knew he could be saved
So I thank you Sisters with all my heart
For I was sent the greatest gift from the start
The Lord is with us, He always will be
We just have to believe and get on our knees
So I thank you Lord, for all you've done
For this man now has only just begun

The Scare

We got the call on Sunday
We couldn't believe our ears
Time stood still in silence
It was a moment we couldn't bear.

You died without us knowing
If only we were there
We'd fight the battle with you
And clear away the scare

We know you're lying peacefully
In our garden we bestow
We love you and we miss you
In our garden now you'll grow

The Virus

We are near the great surge
And far from the volcanic peak
We didn't see it coming here
It was never meant to leak

We scramble to control our plight
It's caught us in our tracks
And no matter where we turn
It seems to be like wax

I haven't given into it
The thought of what's to be
A virus is a funny thing
A fear that will not haunt me

I say this as a friend
Who has experience from the war
Do not surrender your dear self
Or give them power from afar

I ask you to think wisely
Of your future, what's to be
As the power is in your hands
For your mind of this uncertainty

There will be time

Today the world seems grim again
There's a certain quietness to its way
It's almost haunting in its stature
A certain type of evil come to stay

Did I ever think each day would be like Sunday
With a calmness of peace in the air?
Did I ever think I wouldn't hug my own mother
Because of circumstances I've learnt just to bear?

Or did we ever think we'd see the day
Where we are all stuck in
And just allowed to stand from the crowd
With only a two-kilometre-round spin

Yes it's weird to say come what may
As if it were all OK
But we've learnt to cope
Using lots of soap
And better things to come our way

So I ask myself what does my future hold?
Or will I just make a super prediction
So here it goes right on the nose of
happiness that raises a word like fiction

I believe in coffee shops bursting with aromas
Where groups would gather in all their tatter
And build up a mild euphoria
I believe in open marts where people
Would come to greet you
With open arms and displays so fine
Only quality would rise to meet you.

And after all that's said and done
There will be time for love and understanding
The day and night will pass and we'll know
At last that hope has made a landing
Where land was green and forever seen
We'll all have made the journey through
So we'll raise a glass to this country tasked
And take pride in what we do

Thoughts

As I sit alone in the car
I wonder why and contemplate far
For it isn't easy on the young today
Their thoughts and dreams are far away

I sit and watch two very old nuns
And wonder how they had begun
To live a life to serve the Lord
It wasn't easy so I've heard

Thoughts are with us all the time
I believe sometimes it is a crime
They come and go but some might stay
We must withstand and make them gay

The hustle and bustle of the cars going by
Different people in the opposite mind
What are they thinking, where are they going
It's a minefield here, not even knowing

So I can tell you my thoughts tell you my dreams
But what does it matter or what does it seem
Thoughts are just thoughts, they fade away
It's what we do right that makes it OK

A Veteran

When I hear the words 'together forward'
I feel an admiration to follow through
It's a certain kind of mutual agreement
The feeling of loyalty one must do

It's the men and women of today
Whose commitment did not lose their way
They ask for nothing in return
But are always there for your concern

It's not an easy thing to write
In the past they had to fight
To prove they're worthy of their game
And all what's lost it was a shame

But I'm here to make that call
All that's lost is not at all
For the fighting Irish will go on
And forever fighting they will be strong

It's the greatest honour I'm sure
To help a nation with a cure
So something I know that's true
A veteran is certainly there for you

Who Was She

A young girl at twelve felt the calling from her god
Her fascination with missionary work was only to applaud
The devotion to her spiritual life quickly came to stay
As she travelled to Ireland on one fine sunny day

The Sisters of Loretta did welcome her with prayer
But India was calling and her vows were coming near
So in 1931 she swore to God above
Her whole life would be dedicated into spreading love

After the patron saint of missionaries she adapted her new name
And Sister Theresa began teaching in Calcutta as her aim
In 1931 she made her final profession of her vows
And earned the name Mother Theresa so beautifully profound

Being headmistress of the school for twenty years or so
She got a calling from above to help in the slums so low
She wanted to serve the poor purely for the love of God
So she learnt basic medicine and truly got involved

She started outdoor schooling and prayed for volunteers to come
And in 1950 the missionaries of charities she soon begun
For the blind elderly disabled, society did not care
She took it on herself and grasped all one could bear

A converted Hindu temple two years later she bestowed
And gave the poorest of people a dignified letting go
She founded her first leper colony courageously setting up
Later children's home of the immaculate heart never giving up

Mother Theresa's order soon became an international
religious family
Spreading the word globally with love and understanding
Hundreds of convents around the world were known
For Mother Theresa earned acclaim for her tiredless work alone

She was awarded the Nobel Peace Prize in 1979
With sacrifices so great that she was in line
In 1982 she negotiated a break in hostilities in beruit
Where thirty seven children were saved because of her astute

Attending to radiation victims after the Cher noble disaster
came to be
And finding a hospice in New York for Aids sufferers she
could see
Her missionaries of charity operated over six hundred
missions alone
With the hundred and twenty three countries she had too
but grown

In 1997 she died after worsening health
And at the Mother House people flocked around her tomb
She serves as a beacon that represents the rest of humanity
And calling her a saint was exactly what to do

Your life

Did you ever feel like you're on a moving ship
Where the waves are so high you're going under?
Did you ever feel like no one's listening to your pain?
And the voices screaming in your mind sound like thunder

Did you ever want to reach out but were afraid
of the sniggers and the stigmas that it holds?
Did you ever try to forget the great pain
But it came back to haunt you just like a cold.

Well this is the start of your new life
Because you're going to get out, stand up and fight
Line up those problems and head for that walk
Remember there's always someone there for you to talk

Remember depression can only make you stronger
When darkness comes, remember the light will follow too
And even if you don't want to believe it
Just remember, there's always someone thinking about you.

When the tide goes out, it comes back in again
When the evening falls, you'll see the moon
And soon to follow will be the daylight
And you can shift your fear to the undefeatable you

So with bravery comes strength that must not surpass you
So you have a choice to stand still or move
So get up that hill and don't be invisible
Take back your life as it belongs to you.

Your Mind

Do not think less of yourself, you are with humility
Plant a garden in your mind and let it grow
Your heart is where you are and your mind is where you live
Things will never be the same, expect change
It is the dreamer who sometimes stays stagnant
Why force to behave and be happy? Let it flow in all its natural beauty
Take pride in your circumstance for it's moments like these one will look back and cherish
No one knows what lies ahead but one can live in the time of the beating heart
Remember the pain in the world while you are surrounded by comforts
Give often, take less and remember they need it more than you
Look around take deep breaths and remember the feeling of birth
Love yourself, love your neighbour, and be grateful for all you have

Emily

The miracle of being pregnant was a joy
I felt every move that you made
I couldn't believe we were quiet joined together
I was blessed for all the days that I prayed

The day finally arrived I would meet you
I just took one look and I knew
You were a blessing that God had sent to me
And we were matched now forever as two

It comes easy to love someone like Emily
As you know you can love them so much
Looking into your eyes it felt incredible
And a bond that noone could touch

I watched you grow over the years
So many special moments you and I shared
Even though the tears fell at times for us
We held each other tight not making a fuss

Now that your older and independently strong
I must tell you I'm so proud of you too
You're a treasure of a daughter and so beautiful
Now and forever I'll always love you.

Tracy's Acknowledgement

I want to pay gratitude to my father who in my life always taught me to be the best I could be. He always steered me in the right direction with the support of always believing in me.

I want to thank my beautiful daughter Emily for her constant praise of all my work. She is the inspiration in my soul to stay writing.

I would like to thank my gorgeous partner Padraig for always being my critique and pushing me to the next level knowing I could do it. He has believed in me since day one.

I would like to thank Keidi Keating my editor and publisher who came and found me on twitter knowing there was something unique about my writing. She has been a great teacher to me throughout my writing journey. I love her spiritual enlightenment always looking towards the light.

Finally I would like to thank my followers on Facebook, Instagram and twitter for their ongoing support in believing in me and encouraging me to write more. Their positivity I will never forget.

Tracy Connolly's Biography

I would describe myself as a Poetess who wants to connect my soul with the world. I want to help others through my poetry. I can write about anything and that's what you will find in my book. From fiction to real life happenings my poetry becomes alive. I think of my audience and can always feel what they need and want in a poem.

I was a Soldier for 23 years and there are two war hero's on either side of my family. They have been decorated with distinguished service medals from the Congo. Most of my family were army. I've been in the war called Operation Grapes Of Wrath in 1996 and felt the pains of others. I've also been to war-torn Kosovo in 2001. I was proud to be a

United Nations Peacekeeper because I love to help others. I'm now a retired Veteran helping in the hospitals as a Healthcare Assistant. Throughout covid I have spent time working with the emergency services within my community.

I started writing during lockdown and it has given me my poetic voice that was simmering beneath the surface for a long time. I would hope my poetry will always help and comfort others. I've been published on Kilkenny's peoples paper with one of the poems here in my book 'The Bloods'. Its about a famous Irish Battalion. Its always good to remember our history.

You can find some of my videos on Facebook under tracyconnollyspoetrys, Youtube Tracy Connolly

I'm also on twitter @poetsbelief and Instagram poetsbelief